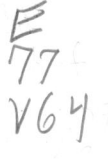

THE INDIAN IN AMERICAN HISTORY

There is a growing interest in the maltreatment of Indians in American history books, and especially in textbooks.[1] It is hardly necessary to expand here on the consequences of such deformed history: the creation or reinforcement of feelings of racial arrogance, and the disgorgement from our schools of students with a warped understanding of their cultural heritage, with no comprehension of the revolutionary changes taking place in the world, and no intellectual equipment for dealing with the problems of race relations here and abroad.

Historians have used four principal methods to create or perpetuate false impressions of aboriginal Americans, namely: *obliteration, defamation, disembodiment,* and *disparagement.* Often the four methods overlap and interlace with one another. Their use does not necessarily flow from conscious malice. More probably, they result from confinement within the narrow limits of the discipline, unfamiliarity with the other social sciences, and the mindsets and assumptions imposed by the historian's own cultural background. The following remarks are based on an examination of more than a hundred books, mainly, but not entirely, designed for use as history texts. Space will permit citing only a few which typify the attitudes we seek to illustrate.

OBLITERATION

Perhaps the chief problem in the historical treatment of American Indians and other minorities is not the biased presentation, but the blackout. We remember that in George Orwell's novel, *1984,* the names of politically disgraced persons were eradicated from the history books. In the language of *newspeak,* they became *unpersons.* To some historians, the American Indian is an unperson, or nearly so. Incredible as it may seem, there are American history books in which the aborigines are nearly or even totally consigned to oblivion. Much of our history has been written by the scribes of the conquerors in the interest of glorification of the winners, and there is little that is glorious in the way they won.

During the nineteenth century the early extermination of the Indian was freely predicted, and even advocated. It is a persistent theme in commentaries of the period, of which Francis Parkman serves as a typical example:

> Their intractable, unchanging character leaves no alternative than their gradual extinction; or the abandonment of the western world to eternal barbarism; and of this and similar plans . . . it may alike be said that sentimental philanthropy will find it easier to cavil at than to amend them.[2]

Although these genocidal aims fell short of accomplishment, the historical obliteration of the Indian was more nearly successful. The treatment of the Jackson era is a revealing case study. One of the cruelest ordeals of the American Indian occurred during the administration of Andrew Jackson and his immediate successor, Martin Van Buren, when more than 125,000 of them were dragged from their homes and deported west of the Mississippi by military force. The "treaties" which preceded these expulsions (94 of them in Jackson's time) were masterpieces of intimidation, bribery, threats, misrepresentation, force, and fraud. Following these efforts to produce a fig-leaf of legality for the operation, Indians were hunted down like animals, bound as prisoners, and confined in stockades to await removal. The conditions of the deportation were so barbarous that about one third of the emigres died on the journey.[3] In the few cases where open resistance was encountered, as with Black Hawk's Sauks, the defiant Indians were massacred.[4]

Jackson also made a farce of the separation of powers in the federal scheme when it did not suit his ends, by encouraging Georgia to violate solemn treaties and to defy the decisions of the Supreme Court in the Cherokee cases.[5] He denied the support of the executive arm to carry out the decisions, while simultaneously threatening to use force against the tariff nullifiers in South Carolina.

Surely such episodes in Old Hickory's administration deserve as much attention as his Maysville veto or his Specie Circular. Yet, in the most widely touted book on the period, *The Age of Jackson*, by Arthur M. Schlesinger, Jr.,[6] there is not one word about the "Trail of Tears" and the "Trail of Death."[7]

To draw the curtain over unpleasant happenings in history is not less to be deplored than conscious falsification. The selectivity of the historian is r e v e a l i n g. If omitted events are of a sort which would dampen the impression the writer seeks to create, we are getting historical fiction, for only novelists can take such liberties. Silence cannot save us from the stain of our Indian policies. Mr. Carleton Beals believed that our acquiescence in Indian dispossession has molded the American character:

> Has not this perhaps led us into demanding no proper accounting from public servants so long as they feed us righteous pap . . . ? Perfect training for later financial plundering . . . the whole ethic of later corporation growth and monopoly—here in the Indian struggle is to be observed the whole American psychology of getting something for nothing, or at most for a little trickery.[8]

Schlesinger has not been exceptional in shutting his eyes to the tragedy of Indian removal. Edward Channing in the nineteenth century praised the Christian concern of the colonists for the Indians' welfare, but his *History of the United States* says nothing about Jackson's Indian policy.[9] Charles and Mary Beard, although seemingly free of racial bias, ignored it in three separate works.[10] W. E. Woodward was blind to Indian removal for, like the Beards, he did not mention Indians in any event later than the year of 1818.[11] Francis Butler Simkins, in his history of the South,[12] also remained silent. Like others, he managed to discuss

---

> Most American history has been written as if history were a function of white culture—in spite of the fact that well into the nineteenth century the Indians were one of the principal determinants of historical events . . . . American historians have made shockingly little effort to understand the life, the societies, the cultures, the thinking, and the feeling of the Indians, and disastrously little effort to uderstand how all these affected white men and their societies.
>
> —Bernard DeVoto, introduction to Joseph K. Howard, *Strange Empire* (New York: Morrow, 1952), p. 8.

South Carolina's quarrel with Jackson over nullification without linking it with the Indian nullification policy of Georgia, with which it was not only contemporaneous, but in the opinion of Commager, Dodd, and others, entirely comparable.[13] Harold Syrett's Jacksonian documents include none of the Tennesseean's messages on Indian removal.[14] Carl Becker failed altogether to mention Indians in his book, *The United States, Experiment in Democracy*.[15]

The Indians of the Old Northwest, who were somewhat less acculturated than their southern brethren, put up a stiffer fight against despoliation. In the 1790's an alliance of these tribes, led by Little Turtle, soundly whipped two armies under Josiah Harmar and Arthur St. Clair before they finally succumbed to Anthony Wayne at Fallen Timbers, and signed the Treaty of Greenville in 1795. A random sampling of ten textbooks (one elementary, one junior high, six senior high, and two college), revealed that these struggles were entirely ignored in half of them, and two others mentioned only Wayne's victory but not the Indian victories preceding it. For some reason Tecumseh, whose efforts to create Indian solidarity were destroyed by Harrison in 1811, has captured the interest of several historians, but almost none of them mention the fate of the Indians in this region after the War of 1812.

DISEMBODIMENT

This school acknowledged the existence of the Indian, but only as a subhuman nomad, a part of the fauna belonging to the wilderness yet to be conquered; in short, a troublesome *obstacle* to be overcome. "We may guess," wrote the Puritan preacher Cotton Mather, "that probably the devil decoyed those miserable savages hither, in hopes that the gospel of the Lord Jesus Christ would never come here to destroy or disturb his *absolute empire* over them."[16] No moral restraint was required in dealing with them. As late as 1872, this attitude found voice in remarks of U.S. Indian Commissioner Francis Walker:

> With wild men, as with wild beasts, the question of whether in a given situation one shall fight, coax, or run, is a question merely of what is easiest and safest.[17]

Accepting the definition of the Indian as less than human, William Bradford in 1620 considered New England to be uninhabited:

> ... the vast and unpeopled countries of America, which are fruitfull & fitt for habitation, being devoyd of all civil inhabitants, where there are only savage & brutish men, which range up and downe, litle otherwise than the wild beasts of the same.[18]

John Smith urged the enslavement of the "viperous brood," which had earlier, he admitted, saved Jamestown from starvation.[19] Benjamin Trumbull held that "as Connecticut abounded in wild animals, so it did also with wild and savage men."[20] If Indians were defined as a kind of animal, it was proper to hunt them as such, and bounties were offered for their scalps, just as for those of wolves.[21] On the far western frontier in the nineteenth century, Indian flesh was eaten, like game.[22]

The view of the Indian as a wild beast in the path of civilization has never died. It was a dominant theme in the treatment of Indians by historians until quite recently. It still lurks in history books in phrases like "Indian menace," "Indian peril," "savage barrier," and "obstacle to settlement." Harold U. Faulkner, in his otherwise commendable book, *American Political and Social History*,[23] listed some cultural contributions of the Indian, but kept old stereotypes alive by calling the Virginia frontier "a constant source of trouble." Indians and loyalists carried on "cruel border warfare" during the revolutionary war, and the frontier generally was "a red line of cruelty." One of the persistent faults in many historians is the inability to see that the whites were also a constant source of trouble to the Indians, and that the Indians, too, were often innocent victims of "cruel border warfare."[24] Not only are massacres of Indians generally overlooked, but also the fact that thousands of Indians were enslaved, some even being shipped to the Barbary States and the West Indies.[25] The "cruelty" stereotype of the Indian needs an examination it seldom gets. Cruelty there sometimes was, but in retaliation for cruelty inflicted, and then hardly worse than the tortures in vogue among whites of that time.[26] The many cases of white captives who were unwilling to return to "civilization" is an eloquent commentary on old images of the Indian.[27]

Indian removal, or slaughter, is customarily presented as the inexorable march of civilization displacing savage hunters. Glyndon G. Van Deusen finds that the white invasion "was deeply resented by the red men, who saw their hunting grounds disappearing before these waves of intruders."[28] The "primitive hunter" myth is the usual expiation for the triumph of brute force. It appears repeatedly in the refrain that "the natives did not develop the land." We deplored the same logic when it was used by Mussolini in Ethiopia. If the right of ownership depended on land use, some wealthy white land owners would today be in jeopardy.

The myth of the Indian as a mere hunter, like many other myths, arises from ignorance concerning the variety of Indian cultures which flourished in America. Most Indians were farmers, and the Southeastern Indians had so far embraced "civilization" by the 1830s that they were known as the "Five Civilized Tribes." The Cherokee had adopted a constitution patterned after that of the United States, and published books and a newspaper in their own language, with Sequoyah's alphabet. A census taken among them in 1825 showed that they owned 33 grist mills, 13 saw mills, 1 powder mill, 69 blacksmith shops, 2 tan yards, 762 looms, 2486 spinning wheels, 172 wagons, 2923 plows, 7683 horses, 22,531 black cattle, 46,732 swine, and 2566 sheep.[29] This adaptation to white concepts of progress, urged upon them by Jefferson,[30] did not save them, but rather accelerated demands for their expulsion.

The inconsistency of Indian removal with alleged civilizing aims was pointed out by Jedidiah Morse, who was commissioned by President Monroe in 1820 to report to Secretary of War Calhoun on the state of the Indians. Morse warned:

> To remove these Indians far away from their present homes . . . into a wilderness among strangers, possibly hostile, to live as their new neighbours live, by hunting, a state to which they have not lately been accustomed, and which is incompatible with civilization, can hardly be reconciled with the professed object of civilizing them.[31]

But the argument persisted that their removal was not only inevitable, but (as a salve for troubled consciences), necessary for their own good. Jackson's claim that "they cannot live in contact with a civilized community, and prosper,"[32] was echoed by historians Louis Hacker and Benjamin Kendrick, who held that "the westward progress of the white man could not be stayed and by the end of the century the Indians were all safely confined on reservations."[33] The notion that "progress" required the nearly complete expropriation of the Indians does not stand up.[34] Indians could have been persuaded, and in fact, before their final expulsion, were persuaded, to live on reduced acreage in their old habitat.[35] Yet, in state after state, in the 1830s and 1840s, the last scraps of land were torn from tribes east of the Mississippi. If greed had been kept within bounds, as it was in Canada, the traumatic effects of forced emigration could have been avoided.

DEFAMATION

This school denigrates the Indian, calls attention to all of his faults and none of his virtues, and condemns him to a status of inferiority in intelligence and adaptability. To this group belongs John Bach McMaster, who may be taken as representative of the late nineteenth-century historians. To him the Indian "was never so happy as when, in the dead of night, he roused his sleeping enemies with an unearthly yell, and massacred them by the light of their burning homes." The Indian was, moreover, only an "idle, shiftless savage." When not hunting or warring, he yielded himself to debauchery, and enslaved his women. His mental attainments,

> were quite of a piece with his character. His imagination was singularly strong, his reason singularly weak. He was as superstitious as a Hottentot negro and as unreasonable as a child.[36]

His contemporary, George Bancroft, blamed the Indians themselves for bringing destruction upon their heads. His judgment was that they would have been treated generously if they had behaved better. Because of their "hasty cruelty" and "inconsiderate revenge" they vanished, "leaving no enduring memorials but the names of rivers and mountains."[37]

To the same school and generation belonged John Fiske, who falsely claimed that New England Indians had been paid for every foot of their land, and, defending the incineration of the Pequots in 1636, maintained that it was wrong "to suppose that savages, whose business is to torture and slay, can always be dealt with according to the methods in use between civilized peoples . . ."[38]

These historians are gone, but their influence is not. Their crude racism has gone out of fashion, but derogation of Indian character continues. In his Pulitzer prize-winning history, R. Carlyle Buley proclaims that "the Potawatomi and the Menominee were . . . a fairly dirty, lazy, and harmless lot."[39] The late David Saville Muzzey, whose books are widely used in high schools, promotes the myth of the nomadic warrior: [the Indians] "were constantly on the warpath, and shifting their hunting grounds."[40] The nomad myth is often used to deny the validity of Indian land claims. Most Indians were in fact less mobile than the current white population.[41] (How many of us were born where we now live?) The Mohawk village of Caughnawaga, Que., is 300 years old this year. Tuscaloosa, Ala., was an Indian village when DeSoto came by in 1540. Oraibi, a Hopi village in Arizona, is the oldest continuously inhabited place in the United States. Tree ring evidence dates it back to 1100 A.D. Therefore, it is older than Berlin or Moscow.

The charge that all Indians were perpetual warriors arises from ascribing Plains Indian customs to all Indians. It is entirely inapplicable to the sedentary Pueblo tribes, and to some Pacific coast and Eastern woodland Indians as well. The role of Indians as peacemakers has been so hidden that a book has been written to rescue this aspect of their history from obscurity, but, like so many of the better books on Indians, it was the work of an "amateur."[42]

DISPARAGEMENT

The fourth way the Indian is scalped by historians is by *disparagement* of, or denial of his extensive contributions to our culture. Richard N. Current and his collaborators declare that "American civilization . . . owed very little to the aborigines of the New World." They further allege that "even the most brilliant of the native cultures were stunted in comparison with the growing civilization of Europe. None of the Indians had an alphabet and . . . none had any conception of the wheel."[43]

The last statement is false; the Aztecs used wheels on children's toys, but had no beasts of burden to enable them to put the principle to better use. But the comparisons made above are perniciously unfair. Barbaric Europe borrowed its wheel and its alphabet, not to mention its numerals and many domesticated plants and animals, from Semitic peoples of Asia. Its gunpowder, compass, and printing press were inventions of Oriental people. Moreover, the argument ignores the instances in which American achievements exceeded those of the Old World: the Maya had a superior calendar and understood the zero before Europe did. Indians domesticated more than forty plants, of which corn is the outstanding example, because it does not and cannot grow wild.[44] In some respects, they excelled in medicine and surgery, e.g., trepanation, and knew the properties of drugs like coca (from whence cocaine), cinchona (from whence quinine), curare, cascara sagrada, and many more. They alone discovered rubber, and with it invented the bulbed syringe. Middle American hieroglyphics, in time, would have evolved into an alphabet.

The remarks of Prof. Current also illustrate the selective criteria which are used to rank cultures into false categories called "higher" and "lower." To measure social advance in our terms reveals an ethnocentric bias. This is ABC to an anthropologist, but not to all historians. We are reminded of a tale, perhaps apocryphal but yet pertinent, that Sitting Bull declared the whites to be "inhuman," because they beat their children, whereas Indians did not.[45] If we measure a society by its non-material culture, which admittedly involves value judgments (as does the material criterion), the Indians might come out ahead. This is the meaning of the opening remarks in John Collier's eloquent book, *The Indians of the Americas*:

> They had what the world has lost. They have it now. What the world has lost, the world must have again, lest it die. . . . It is the ancient, lost reverence and passion for human personality, joined with the ancient, lost reverence for the earth and its web of life.[46]

W. E. Woodward held that the Indians "were singularly lacking in inventive ability, and in the sense of adaptation." He even berated them for not learning how to make whiskey from corn![47] However, Clark Wissler has listed 24 Indian inventions not known in the Old World in 1492, and 16 others known in the Old World which were independently discovered in the New World.[48] There are also many examples of adaptation, such as use of the horse, which transformed the culture of the Plains tribes.[49] Indians were also prompt to adopt guns, metal tools, and a wide range of white trade goods. In fact, their dependence on these commodities was a factor in their downfall.

Entirely forgetting the services of Squanto and other Indians to the Mayflower passengers, Henry Bamford Parkes declared that the Pilgrims discovered how to survive "entirely by their own labors."[50] Even in areas where the Indian has made spectacular contributions, they are denied. Alden T. Vaughan alleges that "the Indians had no bona fide medicine to speak of."[51] In fact, the Indians of North America (north of Mexico) used about 150 medicines which were later included in the U.S. *Pharmacopeia* and *National Formulary*, and the Indians of Latin America contributed about fifty more.[52] Accounts of explorers, from Cartier on, are filled with tributes to Indian medical skill which, although frequently mixed with magic, was considered by many to excel that of Europe at the time.

"Nor have the Indians made any substantial contribution to the civilization that we now have in the United States," comments Oliver Perry Chitwood.[53] To be sure, he admits that the Indians aided the colonists at first. They taught colonists how to clear the land and grow corn and tobacco, acted as guides, procured furs for trade, taught the colonials how to make maple sugar, to hunt and trap, and dress their skins. They showed the white man how to make a bark canoe, and endowed our map with euphonious place names. Yet, he concludes, "aside from these contributions, American life has not been modified by Indian influence."

Unlike earlier writers, Chitwood did not ascribe the retardation of the Indians to racial inferiority. "The race is not lacking in mental vigor," he conceded. Instead, he held that they were handicapped by the lack of beasts of burden and milk cattle, and were cut off from Old World centers of culture from which they could have learned. Nevertheless, he continued, "the fact remains that the aboriginal inhabitants of our part of this continent failed to appreciate and exploit the richest gifts that nature has ever bestowed on any land."

A third of a century has passed since that was written, yet few later historians have advanced beyond the tunnel vision it exhibits. The really comprehensive account of the Indian contributions remains to be written. What we have is mainly the work of anthropologists, and it is not always easily available.[54]

Let us take a closer look at the argument. Chitwood confines his attention to the aborigines of *our part* of this continent. Thus, not a nod or a footnote is accorded to the mighty attainments of the Middle American and Andean civilizations: the Mayan astronomy, mathematics, and architecture, the skillful metal work and other arts of the Aztecs and Incas, the domestication of the turkey, Muscovy duck, honeybee, alpaca, llama, and guinea pig; the roads, communications, scientific land use and political organization of the Incas; the invention of paper and the weaving of cotton cloth in Mexico, and other achievements previously mentioned. To judge Indian attainments by the more limited material progress of those living north of the Rio Grande is as one-sided as if we should measure European civilization by the achievements of the Lapps, or the primitive Germans described by Tacitus, or if we should subtract from Europe's culture all that was borrowed from Asia.[55]

Our Indians, it is said, failed to appreciate and exploit the resources at their disposal. This view fails to consider that the demographic facts caused no pressure for extensive development. Moreover, the Indian use of resources was different from ours. For example, the rivers and lakes were canoe routes and sources of food. We have turned them into foul sewers. The Plains were a hunting ground. There we overcultivated and turned the region into a dustbowl scarred by wind and rain. Recognizing no value in forests except as lumber, we cut them down and unleashed floods in our river valleys. We were so committed to the idea that all of nature's bounty should yield financial gain, that for a long time we failed to appreciate the recreational, ecological, and esthetic value of unspoiled wilderness. The concept of nature as an enemy to be slain lives on in the dogmas of Eric Hoffer. Belatedly we are returning some lands to their wild state, a retreat which would astonish our practical forefathers.

But North American Indians were not averse to resource development. They mined and worked copper, lead, mica, and coal. (Latin American Indians mined gold, silver, tin, platinum, and jade). They discovered oil and made salt by evaporation.[56] Southwestern Indians built irrigation canals, raised cotton, and farmed the land to a near optimum level. Where conditions permitted, North American Indians planted corn, squash, beans, pumpkins, tobacco, sunflowers, and drug plants. They discovered natural dyes which were used by the pioneers, and used hundreds of wild plants for food and medicine.

VI

As Rome hid its debt to the Estruscans, we have obscured our inheritance from the red men. Anthropologists know that acculturation proceeds in both directions when two societies are in any kind of contact, and that even a conquered people helps to shape the destiny of their overlords. "North Americans have maintained the European level with the strictest possible puritanism," wrote psychiatrist Carl Jung, "yet they could not prevent the souls of their Indian enemies from becoming theirs."[57] For our own benefit, let us resurrect some lost truth.

Indians picked the sites now occupied by many of our great cities, and plotted the trails and canoe portages which are followed to this day by our highways, railroads, and canals.[58] We copied their dress, and not only in the fringed buckskin of Daniel Boone. From them we learned to substitute long pants for knee breeches; our women borrowed their feathers and paint, and we wear their moccasins, their parkas, and ponchos.[59] Their beads and bells are popular with our hippies. We smoke their tobacco and eat their foods: the tapioca of the Amazon, the beans, avocados, pineapples, chocolate, peppers, and vanilla of Mexico, the tomatoes, potatoes, and peanuts of

Peru, the cranberries, squashes, and pecans of North America. The pemmican of the Plains Indian has served as food for Antarctic explorers. From the Mexican Indians we borrowed chewing gum, tamales, chili, and tortillas; from our own, hominy, succotash, corn pone, and popcorn.[60]

They have influenced our literature far beyond Cooper's *Mohicans,* and Longfellow's *Hiawatha,* which is our truest national epic. Edna Ferber, Hamlin Garland, Helen Hunt Jackson, and Oliver LaFarge are a few among many who have portrayed the Indian in novels. Thomas Wolfe and Ernest Hemingway used Indian themes in short stories, while Philip Freneau, John Neihardt, Lew Sarett, and Walt Whitman glorified them in poetry.[61] Indian mythology constitutes our most authentic American folk-lore. Appropriately, the first bible printed in this country was in an Algonquian language, John Eliot's *Indian Bible,* (1663).

Indians have influenced composers of music; among those indebted to them are Charles Wakefield Cadman, Anton Dvorak, Anton P. Heinrich, Victor Herbert, Thurlow Lieurance, Harvey W. Loomis, Edward A. McDowell, and Charles S. Skilton.[62]

Their arts and designs have influenced our arts, jewelry, home decoration, and even our architecture.[63] Not only did early settlers imitate the Indian wigwam and palisade, but the Army modified the Plains tepee into the Sibley tent. Today, a prefabricated vacation home in the shape of a tepee, called *Wigwam 70,*[64] has been marketed by the National Design Center in Chicago. The Quonset hut, which is widely used where simplicity is demanded, has both an Indian name and an Indian design. Buckminster Fuller's "geodesic dome" is an aboriginal wigwam covered with metal or glass instead of bark. Our modern skyscrapers copy the terraced setback of the Maya. Pueblo adobe bricks became the white man's building material in the Southwest. The cube style of the Pueblos appears in the LaFonda hotel in Santa Fe, and Moshe Safdie's *Habitat* at Expo '67 in Montreal. Willard Carl Kruger's New Mexico state house is in the shape of the Zia sun symbol. Frank Lloyd Wright acknowledged his debt to the Maya and incorporated their themes in some of his buildings. Of their temples he wrote: "A grandeur arose in the scale of total building never since excelled, seldom equalled by man either in truth of plan or simple integrity of form."[65]

Not only was the Indian a sculptor, but he has inspired our sculptors as well. Leonard Crunelle, Malvina Hoffman, Ivan Mestrovic, and Lorado Taft are among those who have portrayed the Indian in stone and bronze.[66] And let us not forget that authentic American creation, the cigar store wooden Indian. Among painters who made their reputation with Indian subjects are Carl Bodmer, George Catlin, Frederick Remington, and Alfred Miller.

We borrowed Indian inventions, and even used their names for many of them: canoe, kayak, pirogue, cigar, hammock, and toboggan. We use his snowshoes, cradleboard, rubber, pipe, and cigarettes. Some of our youth play LaCrosse and other games evolved from Indian sports.[67] Indian lore enlivens the program of youth organizations. Indian dance clubs and craft groups composed of white adults are flourishing in the United States and Europe.[68] Indian themes are in children's toys and juvenile literature. Indians have long been important in the movies, as they were earlier on the stage,[69] but it has only been recently that they have been portrayed on the screen with sympathy and dignity, in films like *Broken Arrow, Devil's Doorway,* and *Cheyenne Autumn.*

They have enriched our langauge. We use their names for the animals: caribou, chipmunk, cougar, coyote, jaguar, manatee, moose, opossum, raccoon, skunk, and woodchuck. The trees carry their names: catalpa, chinquapin, hickory, papaw, pecan, persimmon, sequoia, tamarack, and tupelo. Some sixty plants have Indian names, including cohosh, puccoon, pipsissewa, and poke. Because of fancy or Indian usage, other plants have names like Indian paint brush, Indian pipe, Indian turnip, moccasin flower, papoose root, and squaw vine. We use their names for topographic features such as muskegs, bayous, and savannas, and speak of hurricanes and Chinook winds. Red men taught us to say hooch, okay, punk, and pewee. From them we borrowed caucus, Tammany, pow-wow, mugwump, podunk, and tuxedo. We have come to use words and phrases like "buck," "bury the hatchet," "go on the warpath," "Indian summer," "Indian giver," "Indian file," "great white father," and "war paint."[70]

We plant Cherokee roses, Catawba grapes, Pima cotton, and Black Hawk raspberries. We drive Pontiac cars and ride in trains called *The Chief* and *Hiawatha.* We call our athletic teams Black Hawks, Braves, Illini, Redskins, and Warriors. We have Cayuse and Appaloosa ponies and Malemute dogs.

From the dispossessed we took the names of twenty-seven states, four of our great lakes, and many of our mountains and rivers, to give, as Mencken said, "a barbaric brilliancy to the American map."[71] Canada and four of its provinces and two of its territories have Indian names, as do ten nations in Latin America. We took Indian names for cities like Chattanooga, Chicago, Kalamazoo, Kenosha, Keokuk, Kokomo, Mankato, Miami, Milwaukee, Muncie, Muskegon, Omaha, Oshkosh, Paducah, Pawtucket, Peoria, Sandusky, Schenectady, Seattle, Sheboygan, Spokane, Tacoma, Tallahassee, Tucson, Tulsa, Waco, and Wichita. Some of their names we translated into colorful English and French equivalents like Bad Axe, Battle Creek, Broken Bow, Medicine Hat, Moose Jaw, Painted Post, and Red Wing; Baton Rouge, Des Plaines, and Fond du Lac.

The Indian brightens our advertising. His totem poles invite us to Alaska, his calendar stone calls us to Mexico. Indians are featured in the advertising of the Santa Fe and Great Northern railroads, and in the tourist advertising of many states. We put an Indian on a baking soda can, on a box of corn starch, on chewing tobacco, patent medicines, and other products. We use their names as trade marks: Black Hawk meats, Cherokee garments, Pequot sheets, Sioux tools, and Wyandotte chemicals. We put the Indian on coins and postage stamps. An Aztec legend is pictured on the Mexican flag, and Indian symbols decorate the state flags of New Mexico and Oklahoma.

The Indian is an important ingredient of our political history. The colonial charters speak of trade and conversion as objects of the colonizers. The Indian presence was a spur to efforts at colonial union, from the New England confederation to the Albany congress. The Iroquois alliance helped to defeat the French, and Indians were significant participants in all colonial wars, and later ones, both as friends and foes. Their rebellion under Pontiac in 1763 won the royal proclamation closing the West to settlement, and launched a chain of events leading to our independence. Indians are mentioned in the Declaration of Independence, the Articles of Confederation, the Northwest Ordinance, the U. S. Constitution, the constitution of the Confederacy, and in numerous presidential messages and party platforms. They figure in at least five treaties with foreign powers.[72] We have made 372 treaties with them and passed over four thousand laws affecting them. Several government agencies are involved with them[73]

Montaigne, Rousseau, and Jefferson paid tribute to the Indian capacity to organize human affairs in a libertarian manner. The Iroquois developed a system of confederated government which, according to Benjamin Franklin, served as an example for his Albany Plan of Union,[74] and eventually for the Articles of Confederation. Felix Cohen has lashed the assumption that our democracy was born in Greece:

> ... it is out of a rich Indian democratic tradition that the distinctive political ideals of American life emerged. Universal suffrage for women as for men, the pattern of states within a state that we call federalism, the habit of treating chiefs as servants of the people instead of their masters, the insistence that the community must respect the diversity of men and the diversity of their dreams—all these things were part of the American way of life before Columbus landed.[75]

The followers of Sam Adams masqueraded as Indians at the Boston Tea Party, and we borrowed Indian military tactics in the revolution, as the poet Robert P. Tristam Coffin has written:

> We bent down to the bob-cat's crouch
> Took color from the butternut tree,
> At Saratoga, Lexington,
> We fought like Indians and went free.

Even customs and folkways: frontier hospitality, and neighborly cooperation, such as barn-raising, were copies of Indian manners. We learned his weather and plant lore. His war whoop was the "rebel yell' in the Civil War, and Tristam Coffin says:
> We even put the pow-wow on,
> We dance the night before we fight,
> Republicans, Democrats, football teams
> With red hot songs build up their might.[76]

The predominant ethnic strain in all but four of the nations of Central and South America is Indian. Indians have shaped the study of anthropology, linguistics, and archaeology, particularly in America, and have contributed to thought in psychology, sociology, law, political theory, and education. They taught us progressive, non-authoritarian ways of rearing and teaching children.[77]

It is a trap to measure the worth of any people by the degree to which they have successfully participated as individuals in a rival culture. Because Indians are few in number and have lived a largely separate life, they cannot point to a large number of such persons. In athletics, however, fame came to Jim Thorpe, Louis Tewanima, Don Eagle, and Charles Albert Bender. In military service, there are Brig. Gen. Eli S. Parker (who wrote the surrender terms at Appomattox), Maj. Gen. Clarence

Tinker, and Rear Admiral Joseph Clark. Indians can point with pride to artists Brummet Echohawk and Beatien Yazz, ballerinas Maria and Marjorie Tallchief, humorist Will Rogers, actor Jay Silverheels (Tonto of the Lone Ranger), William Keeler, executive vice-president of the Phillips Petroleum Corporation, present Indian commissioner Robert Bennett, and Congressman Ben Reifel.[78] Vice-president Charles Curtis boasted of his Indian inheritance.

RECOMMENDED BOOKS

Nowhere can we find a history book that tells more than a small fragment of these things. Some of the unit study books of the elementary schools picture Indians as engaged exclusively in primitive pursuits such as hunting and fishing. The effect is the same as the old image of the Negro as a cotton-picker and watermelon eater.

Although there is no comprehensive account of the Indian cultural contributions, there are some commendable materials available at all levels. For the lower grades we can recommend Tillie Pine's little book, *The Indians Knew* (New York: Whittlesey House, 1957). For middle grades, the Field Museum of Natural History's *Children of Indian America* and *Plants that the American Indians Used*, are superb. The Milwaukee Public Museum has a series of pamphlets in the *Lore Leaves* series, of which *Famous Indian Americans* is one of the best. For the upper grades and high schools, Ruth M. Bronson, *Indians are People Too*, E. Russell Carter, *The Gift is Rich*, and David Munroe Cory, *Within Two Worlds*, all published by Friendship House of New York, emphasize Indian cultural contributions.

One of the better high school texts is Lewis Paul Todd and Merle Curti, *Rise of the American Nation* (New York: Harcourt Brace, 1964). It is notably free of racial bias and shows the Indian side of some frontier struggles. There is a sympathetic portrayal of the peaceful aims of Tecumseh, and an acknowledgement that the Pilgrims at Plymouth "might not have survived had it not been for the help of friendly Indians." But some of the old baggage is retained. We are given a hair-curling account of the Virginia Indian uprising of 1622, without a word about its causes. A picture, entitled "an Indian raid," shows nearly naked savages lurking in the bushes, ready to pounce on a settler's cabin. Father Junipero Serra's "civilizing" mission in California is described, with no hint of the serfdom, oppression, and cultural and physical destruction which the mission Indians suffered, while Spanish troops backed up the authority of the priests.

One world history text for high schools which gives an unusually comprehensive account of the cultural attainments of both the American Indian and non-western civilizations is Thomas W. Wallbank and Arnold Schrier, *Living World History* (Glenview, Illinois: Scott Foresman & Co., 1964).

Of books designed for adult and college readers, James Truslow Adams' somewhat dated *Epic of America* (Boston: Little, Brown & Co., 1937), deserves mention because it portrays the Indian as the victim of English greed and racial arrogance. English racial pride, he indicates, prevented amalgamation with the Indians, such as was common in the French and Spanish colonies. He is almost alone in blaming Harrison for the battle of Tippecanoe, and credits Tecumseh's Indians with high-minded aims.

Perhaps the most nearly flawless college text is Samuel Eliot Morison and Henry Steele Commager's *The Growth of the American Republic* (2 vols.; New York: Oxford University Press, 1962). While some texts begin the history of America with "the European background," this one begins with the native background. Indians are credited with the discovery of the New World, and in truth, it is no more correct to ascribe the discovery of this occupied land to Europeans than it would be to call Roman invaders the discoverers of Britain. The Indians are called "our Mongoloid pilgrim fathers" and the culture they developed is adequately described. It is noted that the Indians were called "nomads" in order to rationalize denial of their title to the land. To these writers Indians were "a great and noble race, which we . . . are proud to claim as predecessors and ashamed to have treated as barbarians, which they were not." They declare that "American culture has been greatly enriched by the Indians' contribution," and "the American charatcer . . . is very different from what it would have been if this continent had been vacant of mankind when our ancestors first arrived." The faithfulness of Indians to treaty stipulations is contrasted with white duplicity and cruelty. They fairly describe the achievements of the Cherokee tribe, and maintain that "they had given as good evidence of worth, and made more progress in civility, than the Georgia crackers who coveted their land." The violations of court decisions involving Cherokee treaty rights by Georgia is called "as clear a case of [defiance of] federal supremacy as that of South Carolina." The diabolical use of whiskey and other devices to extort land cessions from Indians is described here, and ignored almost everywhere else. To the degree that it corrects old myths and omissions, this is clearly a superior book. Commager's *Documents of American History* (7th ed.; New York: Appleton Century Crofts, 1963), is the only book of its type which contains some source material relating to Indian affairs. The earlier editions, however, contain items which are omitted in the latest.

Every teacher should have these valuable resource tools of recent vintage: Harold E. Driver, *The Americas on the Eve of the Discovery* and Jack D. Forbes, *The Indian in America's Past* (both published by Prentice-Hall of Englewood Cliffs, N. J., 1964), and Wilcomb Washburn, the *Indian and the White Man* (Garden City, N. Y.: Doubleday, 1964).

Through books such as these we can begin to reorient our teaching about the Indians, a task which is long overdue.

NOTES

[1] Jeanette Henry, "Our Inaccurate Textbooks," *The Indian Historian*, I, No. 1 (December, 1967), 21-24.

[2] Parkman, *The Conspiracy of Pontiac* (New York: E. P. Dutton, 1908), II, 101.

[3] Best accounts of the removal are Grant Foreman's two books, *Last Trek of the Indians* (Chicago: University of Chicago Press, 1946), which describes the expulsion of the Indians from the Old Northwest, and *Indian Removal* (Norman: University of Oklahoma Press, 1953), which deals with the Southern Indians. Also valuable for the latter is Dale Van Every, *The Disinherited* (New York: Avon Books, 1966).

[4] *Autobiography of Black Hawk*, ed. by Donald Jackson (Urbana: University of Illinois Press, 1955).

[5] The more important Cherokee cases were *Corn Tassel vs. Georgia*, *Cherokee Nation vs. Georgia*, and *Worcester vs. Georgia*. In the last case, in-

volving the arrest of a missionary to the Cherokee by the state of Georgia, the court, headed by John Marshall, ruled that the laws of Georgia were not applicable within the territory of the Cherokee Nation. See Commager, *Documents*, 7th ed., docs, #140 and #141, and D'Arcy McNickle, *They Came Here First* (Philadelphia: J. B. Lippincott, 1949), Chapter XX.

[6] Boston: Little Brown & Co., 1949.

[7] Schlesinger does devote three sentences to the "case of the Georgia missionaries" (p. 350), as an example of how Jackson incurred the ire of religious groups, but says nothing about its effect on the Indians, and nothing about removal.

[8] Beals, *American Earth* (Philadelphia: J. B. Lippincott, 1939), pp. 63-64.

[9] New York: Macmillan, 1928.

[10] *The Making of American Civilization* (New York: Macmillan, 1938), *Basic History of the United States* (Philadelphia: Blakiston, 1944), and *The Rise of American Civilization* (New York: Macmillan, 1956).

[11] Woodward, *A New American History* (New York: Garden City Publishing Co., 1938).

[12] Simkins, *The South, Old and New* (New York: Alfred A. Knopf, 1947).

[13] Samuel E. Morison and Henry S. Commager, *The Growth of the American Republic* (2 vols.; New York: Oxford University Press, 1962), I, 489); William E. Dodd, *Expansion and Conflict* (Boston: Houghton Mifflin Co., 1915), pp. 87-89. See also Woodrow Wilson, *Division and Reunion*, (New York: Longmans Green & Co., 1932), pp. 37-40.

[14] Syrett, *Andrew Jackson, His Contributions to the American Tradition* (Indianapolis: Bobbs Merrill, 1953).

[15] New York: Harper Bros., 1920.

[16] Mather in *Magnalia Christi Americana*, quoted in Alden T. Vaughan, *New England Frontier* (Boston: Little Brown & Co., 1965), p. 20.

[17] Quoted in Jack D. Forbes, ed., *The Indian in America's Past* (Englewood Cliffs, N. J., Prentice-Hall, 1964), p. 113.

[18] Bradford, *Of Plymouth Plantation* (New York: Capricorn Books, 1962), p. 40.

[19] L. G. Tyler, ed., *Narratives of Early Virginia* (New York: Scribner's, 1907), pp. 37-41, 360, 364 ff. "Our provision being now within twentie dayes spent, the Indians brought us great store both of Corne and bread ready made," is one of several tributes Smith earlier paid to Indian generosty.

[20] Trumbull, *A Complete History of Connecticut, 1630-1764* (New London: H. D. Utley, 1898), p. 21.

[21] On scalp bounties, see Emerson Hough, *The Passing of the Frontier* (New Haven: Yale University Press, 1893), p. 134; Bancroft, *History*, I, 128-29; M. W. Stirling, *National Geographic Magazine*, November, 1937, p. 582; Beals, *American Earth*, p. 46; Daniel Boorstin, *The Americans, the National Experience* (New York: Random House, 1966) p. 127. Edward Channing relates that Leonard Calvert and his agent, Giles Brent, advised Maryland colonists to shoot all Indians on sight. (*History*, I, 259). On biological warfare, see Woodward, *A New American History*, p. 106.

[22] Everett Dick, *Vanguards of the Frontier* (New York: D. Appleton Century, 1944), p. 511; Raymond W. Thorp and Robert Bunker, *Crow Killer* (New York: Signet, n.d.), p. 9.

[23] 7th ed.; New York: Appleton-Century-Crofts, 1965, pp. 33, 126.

[24] E.g., the Conestoga, Gnadenhutten, and Sand Creek massacres. See Helen Hunt Jackson, *A Century of Dishonor* (New York: Harper Torchbooks, 1965), Chapters III, IX.

[25] Almon W. Lauber, *Indian Slavery in Colonial Times* (New York: Columbia University Press, 1913).

[26] In Montaigne's view "[we] surpass them in every kind of cruelty." Michel de Montaigne, *Complete Essays* (Stanford: Stanford University Press, 1958), p. 156.

[27] See Cadwallader Colden, *The History of the Five Indian Nations* (Ithaca: Cornell University Press, 1964), pp. 180-81; William Smith, *Expedition Against the Ohio Indians* (Ann Ar-

bor: University Microfilms, 1966), pp. 26-29.

[28] Van Deusen, *The Jacksonian Era* (New York: Harper & Bros., 1959), p. 48.

[29] Albert Gallatin, "Synopsis of Indian Tribes," in *Transactions and Collections of the American Antiquarian Society* (Cambridge, 1836), II, 157.

[30] Address to chiefs of the Cherokee nation, January 10, 1806, in Adrienne Koch and William Peden, *The Life and Selected Writings of Thomas Jefferson* (New York: Modern Library, 1944), pp. 578-80.

[31] Morse, *Report to the Secretary of War on Indian Affairs* (New Haven: S. Converse, 1822), p. 82.

[32] Message on Indian removal, December 7, 1835, in Commager, ed., *Documents*, pp. 259-61.

[33] Hacker and Kendrick, *The United States Since 1865* (New York: F. S. Crofts Co., 1934), pp. 136-38.

[34] In sixteen states, all in the eastern half of the U. S., there is no land in tribal ownership. In New York, however, there are some fair sized reservations, which have hardly inhibited the growth of civilization there. See leaflet, *Indians: Surviving Groups in Eastern States* (Washington: Bureau of Indian Affairs, 1963).

[35] *E.g.*, see Jefferson's reference to the Kaskaskia cession, in his third annual message, in Koch and Peden, *op. cit.*, p. 336.

[36] McMaster, *History of the People of the United States from the Revolution to the Civil War* (New York: Farrar, Straus & Co., 1964), p. 15.

[37] Bancroft, *History of the United States of America* (New York: D. Appleton & Co., 1893), I, 128-29, 165.

[38] Fiske, *The Beginnings of New England* (Boston: Houghton Mifflin Co., 1889), p. 184.

[39] Buley, *The Old Northwest* (2 vols.; Bloomington: University of Indiana Press, 1964), II, 127. *Cf.* the view of the Potawatomi by Pierre-Jean De-Smet, who reported in 1838 that he "had not seen so imposing a sight nor such fine-looking Indians in America." *Life, Letters and Travels of Father Pierre-Jean DeSmet, S.J.* (New York: Francis P. Harper, 1905), I, 157.

[40] Muzzey, *A History of Our Country* (Boston: Ginn & Co., 1957), p. 24.

[41] Henry Henshaw answered the "nomad" myth in his article "Popular Fallacies" in F. W. Hodge, ed., *Handbook of American Indians* (Bureau of American Ethnology, Bulletin 30, 2 vols.; Washington: Government Printing Office, 1907-10, II, 283.

[42] Mabel Powers, *The Indian as Peacemaker* (New York: Fleming H. Revell Co., 1932).

[43] Richard N. Current, T. Harry Williams, and Frank Freidel, *American History, A Survey* (2d ed.; New York: Alfred A. Knopf, 1966), p. 4.

[44] Alphonse de Candolle, *The Origin of Cultivated Plants* (New York: D. Appleton & Co., 1902), *passim*.

[45] Oliver LaFarge, *As Long as the Grass Shall Grow* (New York: Alliance Book Corporation, 1940), p. 7.

[46] Collier, *Indians of the Americas* (New York: W. W. Norton, 1947), p. 15.

[47] Woodward, *A New American History*, pp. 103-4.

[48] Wissler, *Indians of the United States* (Garden City, N. Y.: Doubleday, 1949), p. 295. See also E. Nordenskjoeld, "The American Indian as an Inventor," in A. L. Kroeber and T. T. Waterman, eds., *Sourcebook in Anthropology* (rev. ed.; New York: Harcourt Brace & Co., 1931), pp. 489-505.

[49] Frank G. Roe, *The Indian and the Horse* (Norman: University of Oklahoma Press, 1955).

[50] Parkes, *The American Experience* (New York: Alfred Knopf, 1947), p. 30. *Cf.* Charles and Mary Beard: "From red Indians 'the palefaces' recovered some of the primitive arts of survival which had been lost by the English since their own primitive times." *Basic History*, p. 25.

[51] Vaughan, *New England Frontier,* p. 34.

[52] Virgil J. Vogel, "American Indian Medicine and its Influence on White Medicine and Pharmacology," PhD dissertation, Department of History, University of Chicago, 1966. Abstract in *The Indian Historian,* December, 1967, pp. 12-15.

[53] Chitwood, *A History of Colonial America* (New York: Harper & Bros., 1931), p. 19.

[54] A good short statement is anthropologist A. Irving Hallowell's "The Impact of the Indian on American Culture," in W. D. Wyman and C. B. Kroeber, eds., *The Frontier in Perspective* (Madison: University of Wisconsin Press, 1965), pp. 229-58. Much of the material presented herein is based on Hallowell's inquiry, or inspired by it.

[55] Defending the Indians from the charge of "lacking genius," Thomas Jefferson compared them with north Europeans at the time of Roman contact, and asked, "how many good poets, how many able mathematicians, how many great inventors in arts or sciences, had Europe, north of the Alps, then produced? And it was sixteen centuries after this before a Newton could be formed."—"Notes on Virginia," in Koch and Peden, *op. cit.,* pp. 212-13.

[56] C. A. Browne, "The Chemical Industries of the American Aborigines," *Isis,* XXIII (1935), 406-24.

[57] Jung, *Contributions to Analytical Psychology* (New York: Harcourt Brace & Co., 1928), p. 139.

[58] Archer B. Hulbert, *Indian Thoroughfares* (Columbus: Arthur H. Clark Co., 1902).

[59] "The forecast is for more and more Indian influence on fashion."—Tony Minor, broadcast, WNUS, January 27, 1968. The entire "Feminique" section of the *Chicago Tribune,* October 2, 1967, was devoted to Indian influence on fashions, jewelry, and home decoration.

[60] A. Hyatt Verrill and Otis W. Barrett, *Foods America Gave the World* (Boston: C. C. Page & Co., 1937); Yeffe Kimball and Jean Anderson, *The Art of American Indian Cooking*

(Garden City, N. Y.: Doubleday & Co.; 1965).

[61] Albert Keiser, *The Indian in American Literature* (New York: Oxford University Press, 1933).

[62] Gilbert Chase, *America's Music* (New York: McGraw Hill, 1955), *passim.*

[63] John Burchard and Albert Bush-Brown, *The Architecture of America* (Boston: Little, Brown & Co., 1961), pp. 57, 236, 351-52.

[64] *Tepee* and *wigwam* are the Dakota and Algonquian terms, respectively, for a dwelling. In English, the first term properly belongs to the skin or canvas tents of the Plains tribes.

[65] Wright, *Writings and Buildings* (New York: Meridian Books, 1960), p. 22.

[66] Marian Gridley, *America's Indian Statues* (Chicago: The Amerindian, 1966).

[67] Allan A. MacFarlan, *Book of American Indian Games* (New York: Association Press, 1960)

[68] Robin Richman, "Rediscovery of the Red Man," *Life,* December 1, 1967, pp. 52-71.

[69] Constance Rourke, *The Roots of American Culture* (New York: Harcourt Brace & Co., 1942), pp.60-74.

[70] Mitford Mathews, *Dictionary of Americanisms* (2 vols.; Chicago: University of Chicago Press, 1951), I, 866-80; A. F. Chamberlain, "Memorials of the 'Indian'," *Journal of American Folk-Lore,* XV, No. 17 (April-June, 1902), 107-16; *idem;* "Algonkian Words in American English," *ibid.,* XV, No. 19 (October-December, 1902), 240-67.

[71] H. L. Mencken, *The American Language* (New York: Alfred A. Knopf, 1947), p. 528.

[72] Jay's treaty with Great Britain, 1794; Pinckney's treaty with Spain, 1795; Treat of Ghent, 1814; Treaty of Guadalupe Hidalgo, 1848; Alaska Purchase Treaty, 1867.

[73] Bureau of Indian Affairs, Indian Claims Commission, Indian Arts and

Crafts Board, U. S. Public Health Service, Volunteers in Service to America. On laws and treaties, see Charles Kappler, ed., *Indian Affairs, Laws and Treaties* (4 vols.; Washington: Government Printing Office, 1903-29).

[74] "It would be a very strange thing, if *Six Nations* of ignorant savages should be capable of forming a scheme for such a union, and be able to execute it in such a manner, as that it has subsisted for ages, and appears indissoluble; and yet that a like union should be impracticable for ten or a dozen *English* colonies, to whom it is more necessary and must be more advantageous, and who cannot be supposed to want an equal understanding of their interests." Franklin to Mr. Parker, March 20, 1751, in John Bigelow, ed., *The Complete Works of Benjamin Franklin* (New York: G. P. Putnam's Sons, 1887), II, 219.

[75] Cohen, "Americanizing the White Man," *The American Scholar*, XXI, No. 2 (Spring, 1952), 179-80.

[76] Both verses from "We Put the Feathers on," in R. P. Tristam Coffin, *Primer for America* (New York: Macmillan Co., 1943), pp. 54-55

[77] Wayne Dennis, *The Hopi Child* (New York: John Wiley, 1965); Robert J. Havighurst and Bernice Neugarten, *American Indian and White Children* (Chicago: University of Chicago Press, 1955).

[78] Marian Gridley, *Indians of Today* (3d ed.; Chicago: Indian Council Fire, 1960).

The American Indian Influence on American Civilization:

A Bibliography

This is not a bibliography for specialists, but for all persons, including teachers, who wish to broaden their knowledge of a neglected subject. It is limited to one aspect: the aboriginal influence on ourselves, and thus excludes most of the literature dealing with Indians. Within this scope, it is not comprehensive, but selective, for economy's sake. Those with more extensive interests will find bibliographies included in many of the works listed. Some specialized bibliographies are also listed herein. Suggestions and additions are invited for possible future use.

I. *The Indian Impact on our Culture*: General Treatment

Brown, Francis J., and Roucek, Joseph S., eds. *One America* (3d ed.; New York: Prentice-Hall, 1952). Includes chapter by Robert F. Heizer on "The American Indian: Background and Contributions." Second edition (1945) includes similar chapter by Clark Wissler.

Carter, E. Russell. *The Gift is Rich* (New York: Friendship Press, 1955). Covers the field, and is so written as to be digestible to high school students, yet interesting to mature scholars.

Chamberlain, Alexander F. "The Contributions of the American Indian to Civilization," *Proceedings of the American Antiquarian Society*, XVI, new series (October, 1903), pp. 91-126. The pioneer study which inspired others.

Cohen, Felix, "Americanizing the White Man," *The American Scholar*, XVI, No. 2 (Spring, 1952), pp. 177-91. The Indians' fighting lawyer pokes a sharp pen at white ignorance of Indian gifts.

Davis, Emily C. *Ancient Americans* (New York: Henry Holt & Co., 1931), Chapter 18 (pp. 272-82): "We owe these to the Indians."

Driver, Harold E. *Indians of North America* (Chicago: University of Chicago Press, 1965), Chapter 26 (pp. 583-612): "Achievements and Contributions."

........, "The Contributions of the Indians to Modern Life," in Driver, ed., *The Americas on the Eve of the Discovery* (Englewood Cliffs, N. J.: Prentice-Hall, 1964), pp. 165-74.

Edwards, Everett E., "American Indian Contributions to Civilization," *Minnesota History*, XV, No. 3 (September, 1934), pp. 255-72. by an agricultural economist with USDA, especially strong in treatment of Indian contributions to the world food supply.

Frachtenberg, Leo. J. "Our indebtedness to the American Indian," *Wisconsin Archeologist*, XVI, No. 2 (July, 1915), pp. 64-69. Reprinted from *Quarterly Journal of the Society of American Indians*, II, 197-202.

Hallowell, A. Irving. "The Impact of the American Indian on American Culture," *American Anthropologist*, LIX, No. 2 (April, 1957), n.s., pp. 201-17. One of the best treatments, by a noted anthropologist.

.... "The Backwash of the Frontier: The Impact of the Indian on American Culture," in Clifton B. Kroeber and Walker D. Wyman, eds., *The Frontier in Perspective* (Madison: University of Wisconsin Press, 1965). Substantially the same as preceding item.

Locke, Alain and Stern, Bernard J. *When Peoples Meet* (New York: Progressing Education Association, 1946), chapter by Clark Wissler on "Our Culture Debt to the Indians."

Richman, Robin. "Rediscovery of the Red Man," *Life*, December 1, 1967, pp. 52-72. Shows the Indian influence in foreign countries and on our hippies.

Rourke, Constance. *The Roots of American Culture* (New York: Harcourt Brace, 1942), Indian influence on theater, pp. 60-74; Indians as artists subjects, pp. 286-87; influence of Indian beliefs in Salem witchcraft episode, p. 20.

Safford, W. E. "Our Heritage from the Indians," *Annual Report of the Board of Regents of the Smithsonian Institution* . . . for the year ending June 30, 1926 (Washington: Government Printing Office, 1927), pp. 405-10. Strong on medicines, drugs, foods.

Walker, Edwin F. "America's Indian Background," *Masterkey*, XIX (1945), pp. 7-13, 83-88, 119-25.

Wissler, Clark. *Indians of the United States, Four Centuries of their History and Culture* (Garden City, N. Y.: Doubleday, 1949), Chapter XIX (pp. 251-56). "When the White Man Went Indian", Chapter XXII (pp. 292-97), "Did the Indian Live in Vain?"

II. *Agriculture and Food*

De Candolle, Alphonse. *Origin of Cultivated Plants* (New York: D. Appleton & Co., 1892). Also 2d ed., 1902. Pioneer work, lists some forty plants domesticated by Indians.

Edwards, Everett E. *A Bibliography on the Agriculture of the American Indians*, compiled with assistance of Wayne D. Rasmussen, U. S. Dept. of Agriculture, Misc. Pub. no. 447, (Washington: 1942).

Gilmore, Melvin R. "Uses of Plants by Indians of the Missouri River Region." 33d *Annual Report of Bureau of American Ethnology*, 1911-12 (Washington: Government Printing Office, 1919), pp. 43-154. Postulates American origin for watermelon.

Kimball, Yeffe, and Anderson, Jean. *The Art of American Indian Cooking* (Garden City, N. Y.: Doubleday, 1965). Indian foods.

Verrill, A. Hyatt, in collaboration with Barrett, Otis W. *Foods America Gave the World* (Boston: C. C. Page Co., 1937). Comprehensive.

III. *Arts, Architecture, and Sculpture*

Bossom, Alfred C. "New Styles of American Architecture and what we Might Learn from the Mayas," *World's Work*, LVI (June, 1928), pp. 189-95.

Burchard, John, and Bush-Brown, Albert. *The Architecture of America* (Boston: Little-Brown & Co., 1961). Scattered references.

Colton, Amy R. "The Red Man's Contribution to our Household Art," *Garden and Home Builder*, XLIV (September, 1926), pp. 31, 62, 74.

Covarrubias, Miguel. *The Eagle, The Jaguar, and the Serpent*. (New York: Alfred Knopf, 1954).

Douglas, Frederic H., and D'Harnoncourt. *Indian Art of the United States* (New York: The Museum of Modern Art, 1941).

Eastman, Charles. "The Indians' Contribution to the Art of America," *Red Man*, VII (December, 1914), pp. 133-40.

Gridley, Marion E. *America's Indian Statues*, (Chicago: The Amerindian, 1966).

McCracken, Harold. *Portrait of the Old West* (New York: McGraw Hill, 1952. Deals with painters of Indian subjects.

Morgan, Lewis H. *Houses and House-Life of the American Aborigines*, (Chicago: Phoenix Books, US Press, 1965). The relationship between house-style and social life.

Quimby, C. *Indians of the Western Frontier* (Chicago: Chicago Field Museum of Natural History, n.d.). Reproductions of the paintings of George Catlin.

Taft, Robert. *Artists and Illustrators of the Old West* (New York: Scribner's, 1953).

Vaillant, George C. *Indian Arts in North America* (New York: Harper Bros., 1939).

Waterman, T. T. "The Architecture of the American Indians," in A. L. Kroeber and T. T. Waterman, eds., *Source Book in Anthropology* (rev. ed.; New York: Harcourt Brace & Co., 1931), pp. 512-24.

Wright, Frank Lloyd. *Writings and Buildings* (New York: Meridian Books, 1960), Maya influence, pp. 21-23, 302. See also plates.

IV. *Costume and Dress*

Warwick, Edward, and Pitz, Henry C. *Early American Costume* (New York: Century Co., 1929).

Wilcox, R. Turner. *Five Centuries of American Costume* (New York: Charles Scribner's Sons, 1963).

Chicago Tribune, October 2, 1967, Feminique section.

V. *Education, child care*

Dennis, Wayne. *The Hopi Child* (New York: John Wiley, 1965).

Havighurst, Robert J. *Education* (Boston: Little, Brown, 1968), chapter on The Hopi Indians.

........, and Neugarten, Bernice. *American Indian and White Children* (Chicago: University of Chicago Press, 1955).

Pettit, G. A. "Primitive Education in North America," *University of California Publications in American Archaeology and Ethnology*, XLIII (1946), pp. 1-182.

VI. *Games and Sports*

Culin, Stewart. "Games of the North American Indians," *24th Annual Report, Bureau of American Ethnology*, 1902-3 (Washington: Government Printing Office, 1907).

MacFarlan, Allan A. *Book of American Indian Games* (New York: Association Press, 1958).

VII. *Inventions and Industries*

Adney Edwin T., and Chapelle, Howard I. *The Bark Canoes and Skin Boats of North America,* pubn. of Smithsonian Institution, Museum of History and Technology (Washington: Government Printing Office, 1964).

Appy, E. P. "Ancient Mining in America," *American Antiquarian and Oriental Journal*, XI (January-November, 1889), pp. 92-99.

Browne, C. A. "The Chemical Industries of the American Aborigines," *Isis*, XXIII (1935), pp. 406-24.

Griffin, James B., ed. *Lake Superior Copper and the Indians*, miscellaneous studies of Great Lakes prehistory (Ann Arbor: University of Michigan Press, 1961).

Nordenskjold, E. "The American Indian as an Inventor," in Kroeber & Waterman, eds., *Sourcebook in Anthropology* (1931), pp. 489-505.

Stone, Doris, and Balser, Carlos. *Aboriginal Metalwork of Lower Central America* (Chicago: Field Museum of Natural History, 1967).

VIII. *Influence on Language*

Chamberlain, Alexander F. "Algonkian Words in American English: a Study in the Contact of the White Man and the Indians," *Journal of American Folk-Lore*, XV, No. 19 (October-December, 1902), p. 240-267.

.... "Memorials of fhe Indian," *Journal of American Folk-Lore*, XV, No. 17 (April-June, 1902), pp. 107-16.

Mathews, Mitford. *Dictionary of Americanisms* (2 vols.; Chicago: University of Chicago Press, 1951), pp. 866-80, *et passim.*

Mencken, H. L. *The American Language* (New York: Alfred A. Knopf, 1947), *passim.*

IX. *Law and Political Theory*

Baudin, Louis. *A Socialist Empire, The Incas of Peru.* (Princeton, N. J.: D. Van Nostrand Co., 1961).

Engels, Frederick. *The Origin of the Family, Private Property and the State* (Chicago: Charles H. Kerr & Co., 1902). Based on Morgan's *Ancient Society, infra.*

Hargrett, Lester. *A Bibliography of the Constitutions and Laws of the American Indians* (Cambridge: Harvard University Press, 1947).

Hoebel, E. Adamson. *The Law of Primitive Man.* (Cambridge: Harvard University Press, 1967).

........, and Llewellyn, Karl N. *The Cheyenne Way. Conflict and Case Law in Primitive Jurisprudence* (Norman: University of Oklahoma Press, 1961).

Lowie, Robert H. *Some Aspects of Political Organization among the North American Aborigines* (London: Royal Anthropological Society, 1948).

Morgan, Lewis H. *Ancient Society* (Chicago: Charles H. Kerr & Co., 1877).

Peterson, H. L. "American Indian Political Participation," *Annals of American Academy of Political and Social Sicence,* CCCXI (1957), pp. 116-26.

Powers, Mabel. *The Indian as Peacemaker,* (New York: Fleming H. Revell Co., 1932).

X. *Influence on Literature*

Brinton, Daniel G. *Aboriginal American Authors* (Philadelphia: 1883).

Dorson, Richard M., ed. *America Begins* (New York: Pantheon, 1950), Chapters 4, 5, 6, 7.

Field, Rachel. *American Folk and Fairy Tales* (New York: Charles Scribner's, 1943).

Fiedler, Leslie L. *The Return of the Vanishing American* (New York: Stein & Day, 1968).

Gridley, Marion E. *Indian Legends of American Scenes* (Chicago: M. A. Donohue, 1939).

Keiser, Albert. *The Indian in American Literature* (New York: Oxford University Press, 1933).

Pearce, Roy H. *The Savages of America.* (Baltimore: Johns Hopkins Press, 1953).

Russell, J. A. *The Indian in American Literature,* 1775-1875, summary of dissertation (Ithaca, N. Y., 1932).

Sarett, Lew. *The Collected Poems of Lew Sarett* (New York: Henry Holt & Co., 1941).

Skinner, Charles M. *Myths and Legends of our Own Land* (Philadelphia: Lippincott, 1896).

Untermeyer, Louis, ed. *American Poetry, from the beginning to Whitman.* (New York: Harcourt Brace, 1931), two poems by Phillip Freneau, also, "American Indian Poetry," pp. 687-704.

Williams, Mentor L. *Schoolcraft's Indian Legends* (East Lansing, Michigan State University Press, 1957).

XI. *Medicine, Drugs, and Psychology*

Adams, William R. "Aboriginal American Medicine and Surgery," *Proceedings of Indiana Academy of Science,* LXI (1951), (Indianapolis: 1952), pp. 49-53.

Brooks, Harlow. "The Medicine of the American Indian," *Bulletin of the New York Academy of Medicine,* 2d ser., V, No. 6 (June, 1929), pp. 509-37.

.... "The Medicine of the American Indian," *Journal of Laboratory and Clinical Medicine,* XIX, No. 1 (October, 1933), pp. 1-23.

Corlett, William T. *The Medicine Man of the American Indian* (Springfield, Ill.: C. C. Thomas, 1935).

Fenton, William H. "Contacts Between Iroquois Herbalism and Colonial Medicine," *Annual Report Smithsonian Institution* for 1941 (Washington: Government Printing Office, 1942), pp. 503.26).

Hrdlicka, Ales. "Disease, Medicine and Surgery Among the American Aborigines," *Journal of the American Medical Association,* XCIX, No. 20 (November 12, 1932), pp. 1661-66.

LaBarre, Weston. "Primitive Psychotherapy in Native American Cultures," *Journal of Abnormal and Social Psychology*, XLII, No. 3 (July, 1947), pp. 294-309.

Jung, Carl. *Contributions to Analytical Psychology* (New York: Harcourt Brace & Co., 1928), pp. 136-40.

Krogman, Wilton M. "Medical Practices and Disease of the Aboriginal American Indians," *Ciba Symposia*, I No. 1 (April, 1939), pp. 11-18.

Mahr, August C." Materia Medica and Therapy among the North American Forest Indians," *Ohio State Archaeological and Historical Quarterly*, LX, No. 4 (1951), pp. 331-54.

Major, Robert C. "Aboriginal American Medicine North of Mexico,' *Annals of Medical History*, n.s., X, No. 6 (November, 1938), pp. 534-49.

Stone, Eric. *Medicine Among the American Indians* (New York: Hafner Publishing Co., 1962).

.... "Medicine Among the Iroquois," *Annals of Medical History*, n.s., VI, No. 6 (November, 1934), pp. 529-39.

Sturtevant, William C. *Bibliography on American Indian Medicine and Health* (Washington: Smithsonian Institution, 1962), mimeo.

Vogel, Virgil J. "American Indian Influence on Medicine and Pharmacology," dissertation abstract, University of Chicago, *The Indian Historian*, I, No. 1 (December, 1967), pp. 12-15.

Wallace, Anthony F. C. "Dreams and Wishes of the Soul: A Type of Psychoanalytic Theory among the 17th Century Iroquois," *American Anthropologist*, n.s., LX, No. 2 (April, 1958), pp. 234-48. Reprinted as "Psychoanalysis among the Iroquois of New York State" in Driver, *Americas on the Eve of the Discovery*, pp. 69-79.

Youngken, H. W. "Drugs of the North American Indians," *American Journal of Pharmacy*, Pt. I, XCVI (July, 1924), pp. 485-502; Pt. II, XCVII (March, 1925), pp. 158-85; Pt. III, XCVII (April, 1925), pp. 257-71.

XII. *Influence on Music*

Chase, Gilbert. *America's Music, From the Pilgrims to the Present*. (New York: McGraw Hill Book Co., 1955), Chapter 20 on Indian tribal music, and scattered references to composers using Indian themes; see index.

Howard, John Tasker. *Our American Music, Three Hundred Years of It*. 3d ed. rev.; New York: Thomas Y. Crowell, 1954), pp. 613-22 on Indian music, and scattered references to influence on composers; see index.

XIII. *Place Names*

Becker, Donald W. *Indian Place Names in New Jersey* (Cedar Grove, N. J.: Phillips-Cambell Pub. Co., 1964). Lacks original research.

Kenny, Hamill. *Indian Place Names of Maryland* (Baltimore: Waverly Press, 1961). Linguistic, rather than historical approach.

Kuhm, Herbert W. "Indian Place-Names in Wisconsin," *The Wisconsin Archeologist*, XXXIII, Nos. 1-2 (n.s., March and June, 1952). Does not evaluate conflicting claims.

Sealock, Richard B., and Seely, Pauline A. *Bibliography of Place-Name Literature, United States & Canada* (2d ed.; Chicago: American Library Association, 1967), see "Indian names" in index. Periodical supplements in *Names* magazine.

Stewart, George R. *Names on the Land*. (New York: Random House, 1945), scattered references to Indian names; some conclusions dubious.

Tooker, William W. *The Indian Place-Names on Long Island* (Port Washington, N. Y.: Ira J. Friedman, 1962). Reprint of a pioneer work in the field.

Vogel, Virgil J. *Indian Place Names in Illinois* (Springfield: Illinois State Historical Society, 1963), Reprint, with slight changes and additions, of four articles published in *Journal of the Illinois State Historical Society*, LV, Nos. 1, 2, 3, 4 (1962).

XIV. Indian Trails: influence on roads, railroads, canals, city sites.

Bolton, Reginald P. *Indian Paths in the Great Metropolis* (New York: Museum of the American Indian, Indian Notes & Monographs, No. 23, 1922). How streets of New York City followed Indian trails.

Dunbar, Seymour. *A History of Travel in America* (New York: Tudor Publishing Co., 1937).

Hulbert, Archer B. *Indian Thoroughfares* (Cleveland: Arthur H. Clark, 1902). Second volume of a 16 volume work.

Meyer, William E. "Indian Trails of the Southeast," *Annual Report, Bureau of American Ethnology*, 1924-25 (Washington: Government Printing Office, 1928).

XV. Miscellaneous categories

Beals, Carleton. *American Earth, the Biography of a Nation.* (Philadelphia: Lippincott, 1939). Fair portrayal of the Indian role in American history.

Collier, John. *Indians of the Americas* (New York: W. W. Norton, 1947). Abridged ed., paper, Mentor, 1948. Sympathetic historical account by U. S. Commissioner of Indian Affairs, 1933-45.

Driver, Harold E. *The Americas on the Eve of the Discovery* (Englewood Cliffs, N. J.: Prentice Hall, 1964), Anthology of articles by anthropologists.

Embree, Edwin R. *Indians of the Americas* (Boston: Houghton Mifflin, 1939). Plea for cultural diversity, "a pageant of peoples."

Farrand, Livingston. *Basis of American History* (New York: Harper, 1904). Vol. II of *The American Nation* series, ed. by A. B. Hart. Anthropologist treats Indian cultural influence.

Forbes, Jack D. *The Indian in America's Past.* (Englewood Cliffs, N. J.: Prentice Hall, 1964). Documentary anthology, first rate.

Gridley, Marion E. *Indians of Today* (3d ed.; Chicago: Indian Council Fire, 1960). Thumbnail biographies of dozens of American Indians who have become successful in the rival culture.

Hodge, Frederick W. ed. *Handbook of American Indians North of Mexico,* Bulletin 30, Bureau of American Ethnology (2 vols.; Government Printing Office, 1907-19). Recently reissued by Pageant Press of New York. An encyclopedia of information, indispensable.

Hodge (previous item) also reissued in facsimile by Rowman and Littlefield of New York, 1965.

Kroeber, A. L. *Cultural and Natural Areas of Native North America* (Berkeley: University of California Press, 1939). Shows the diversity of native cultures, and their ecology.

Lauber, Almon W. *Indian Slavery in Colonial Times Within the Present Limits of the United States* (New York: Columbia University & Longmans Green, 1913). Doctoral dissertation dealing exhaustively with a little-known feature of American history.

Martin, Paul S., Quimby, George I., and Collier, Donald. *Indians Before Columbus* (Chicago: University of Chicago Press, 1947). A good introduction to American archaeology, which is shipped by aboriginal prehistory.

McNickle, D'Arcy. *They Came Here First, the Epic of the American Indian* (Philadelphia: Lippincott, 1949). The Indian role in our history, written by an Indian.

........., and Fey, Harold E. *Indians and other Americans* (New York: Harper, 1959). The Indians today, and their problems.

Mohr, Watler H. *Federal Indian Relations, 1774-88* (Philadelphia: the author, 1933). Ph.D. dissertation showing the role of the Indian as friend and foe during the revolutionary war period.

Radin, Paul. *Primitive Man as Philosopher* (New York: Dover Publications, 1957), Reprint of a classic.

Steiner, Stan. *The New Indians* (New York: Harper & Row, 1968). The rising tide of protest among today's Indians. Indispensable to anyone who wants to know what is going on.

Turner, Frederick J. *The Frontier in American History* (New York: Henry Holt, 1958). Chapter I, especially, shows how Indian ways were necessarily followed by the early settlers.

Washburn, Wilcomb E. *The Indian and the White Man* (Garden City, N. Y.: Doubleday-Anchor, 1964). First rate documentary anthology.

Weeden, William B. *Indian Money as a Factor in New England Civilization* (Baltimore: Johns Hopkins, 1884). Wampum was legal tender in colonial days.

Wertenbaker, Thomas J. *The First Americans* 1607-1690 (New York: Macmillan Co., 1927), pp. 308-10. Brief treatment of Indian influence on life and customs of colonists.

Wissler, Clark. *The American Indian* (Gloucester: Peter Smith, 1957). Reprint of his earlier work, a treasury of information.

XVI. *Periodicals*

The Indian Historian. Quarterly journal of the American Indian Historical Society, 1451 Masonic Ave., San Francisco, Calif., 94117. Annual subscription: $3.50.

Ethnohistory. Quarterly journal of the American Society for Ethnohistory SUNY at Buffalo, 205 Foster Hall, Buffalo, N. Y. $5 per annum.

Indian Voices. Robert K. Thomas, editor, 1126 E. 59th St. (University of Chicago), Chicago, Ill. 60637. Publication aim: bi-monthly. $3.50 per year.

The issues of February and April, 1964 contain extensive lists of publications issued by tribes, Indian organizations, and Indian interest groups. A similar list (though shorter) is contained in Stan Steiner's *New Indians* (supra), pp. 295-96.

XVII. *Bibliographies* (see others under specific topical headings above)

Dockstader, Frederick J. *The American Indian in Graduate Studies.* New York: Museum of the American Indian, Heye Foundation, 1957). Lists all known MA theses and PhD disertations dealing with Indians, up to the date of publication.

Gallagher, James J. *An Annotated Bibliography of Anthropological Materials for High School Use* (New York: Macmillan, 1967). Not limited to Indians, but world-wide in scope.

Gibson, G. D. "A Bibliography of Anthropological Bibliographies: The Americas," *Current Anthropology,* I (1960), pp. 61-75.

Hagan, William T. *The Indian in American History.* Publication no. 50, service center for teachers of history, American Historical Association (New York: Macmillan, 1963). Has useful commentary.

Murdock, George P. *Ethnographic Bibliography of North America* (3d ed.; New Haven: Human Relations Area Files, 1960). An extensive compilation, arranged by geographical regions.

Rouse, Irvin, and Goggin, John M. *An Anthropological Bibliography of the Eastern Seaboard* (New Haven: Eastern States Archaeological Federation, 1947).

Bibliography of the History and Prehistory of Indians of the Chicago Region. A brief, selected list, available from the compiler of the present bibliography.

University of Oklahoma Press, current publication lists, especially "Civilization of the American Indian" series.

Bureau of Indian Affairs Dept. of the Interior, various publications.

Bureau of American Ethnology, bulletins and annual reports. (Now merged with its sponsor, the Smithsonian Institution).

Publication list of the Public Museum of the City of Milwaukee.

Publication list of the Museum of the American Indian, Heye Foundation, New York City.